T0208724

Persecuted
But Still
Standing

Persecuted
But Still
Standing

Pastor Charlene Evans Morton

WESTBOW°
PRESS
A DIVISION OF THOMAS NELSON
& ZONDERVAN

WestBow Press books may be ordered through
booksellers or by contacting:

WestBow Press
A Division of Thomas Nelson & Zondervan
1663 Liberty Drive
Bloomington, IN 47403
www.westbowpress.com
1 (866) 928-1240

Because of the dynamic nature of the Internet, any web addresses or
links contained in this book may have changed since publication and
may no longer be valid. The views expressed in this work are solely those
of the author and do not necessarily reflect the views of the publisher,
and the publisher hereby disclaims any responsibility for them.

Scripture taken from the Holy Bible, NEW INTERNATIONAL
VERSION®. Copyright © 1973, 1978, 1984 by Biblica, Inc.
All rights reserved worldwide. Used by permission. NEW
INTERNATIONAL VERSION® and NIV® are registered trademarks
of Biblica, Inc. Use of either trademark for the offering of goods or
services requires the prior written consent of Biblica US, Inc.

Images by Dannie Daniel.

ISBN: 978-1-4908-4969-0 (e)
ISBN: 978-1-4908-4968-3 (sc)

Library of Congress Control Number: 2014917003

Printed in the United States of America.

WestBow Press rev. date: 9/30/2014

CONTENTS

My Childhood 1

Testimony 20

The Death of My Daughter 24

My Brother Dennis 44

Betrayal 47

The Church 52

Leadership 70

Broken but Still Standing 76

Healings and Miracles 87

Funny Stories 107

Favorite Proverbs 111

ACKNOWLEDGMENTS

I was inspired to write this book many years ago, but I just didn't do it. A classmate, Ronald Maloney, invited me to his book signing. I called another classmate, and we went to the library for the event. As he shared the details of his book *Powerhouse Road*, something leaped in my belly.

I knew it was time for me to birth this book. Thank you, Ronnie, for inspiring me to get moving and doing what needed to be done.

I began writing short stories of my life over twenty years ago. But I couldn't write this book before, because I had stories that had not yet transpired. Now is the time to put them all together. I realize timing is critical when sharing life events.

MY CHILDHOOD

What is a childhood? That word is foreign to me; I never had one. I was the oldest girl born to Walter "Mid" and Zelma "Doll" Evans. There were five siblings under me: Ronnie, Sylvia, Dale, "Nita," Randall. I also had an older brother, "Woogie."

I became the mother figure for the last four siblings. I began cooking at twelve. Our mother was a good cook—when she decided to cook.

My parents got married in 1950 or 1951. My brother was in the oven and was born in 1951. My aunt once told me when my mother married my daddy she had a box of shoes and clothes. How many young black girls in the early fifties had a box of shoes? I'm told Granddaddy may have been in the moonshine business. I don't know if that is true, but if it is, he had the money to buy her whatever she wanted. She was his only biological daughter and he spoiled her.

Her spoiled behavior carried into adulthood. When we became teenagers, our mother bought clothes for herself first and then for us. Because of that, I always bought for my children first and myself last. Being the oldest girl, I always got the new dress and passed it down to my younger sisters. When I look at our childhood pictures, our Mother always had us dressed nicely when we went to church.

Our parents came from strict homes, but they were not as strict with us. I learned quickly that children need boundaries. The Bible says when we discipline our children, we are telling them we love them and want the best for them.

Getting back to my childhood, I became the maid in the house. I did it all—cooked, cleaned, and scrubbed the floors. My daddy and brother made me cry when they walked on the still-wet floor after I scrubbed it. They devalued what I had done. My work to keep the house clean meant nothing to them. To this day, when I go into a store, I can't stand to walk on a wet floor.

So I tiptoe around it. It's amazing what sticks with you from childhood.

I also had to wash diapers. I hated it. I used to think, *These are not my children. My momma should be doing this.* When Pampers came out, I vowed I would never put a cloth diaper on my children. And I didn't. I only used Pampers; I didn't care how much they cost. After all, I was working. I did, however, buy a dozen cloth diapers to use for burping the baby.

When I became twenty, I resented the fact I never had a childhood. I had to do what my mother should have been doing. I made sure my siblings did their homework. I laid out their clothes and did their hair.

Once, after I had gotten married and had my own children, my mother whipped my sister. My sister called me and said, "Mom just whipped me." I said, "She is your mother." I realized then they saw me as the mother figure because they would move when I spoke to them.

My mother took me to the laundry and left me there to do the wash. In the beginning, she put the clothes in the washer and started it. But once I got the hang of it, she would just set out the baskets. I washed and folded the clothes neatly. She gave me twenty dollars to do the wash. I was fourteen years old and liked that she paid me for my work. Sometimes I was the only one in the laundry, waiting for her to come and get me.

When I turned sixteen and began driving the school bus, I realized there was a reason she gave me the money. It was hush money. My daddy thought she was with me at the laundry, but I was at the laundry two to three hours by myself.

I decided I was not going to do it anymore. I had my own money, so I told Daddy what she had done and asked him not to tell her. I thought he had my back, but he threw me under the bus.

They argued about what she had done. He yelled, "Charlene told me you have been leaving her at the laundry by herself." He asked her where she had been going, as if he didn't know. I had figured it out by then. I was in my room, thinking, *What is he doing? She's going to hate me.* What was wrong with my daddy? He knew she would be mad at me. You can believe I never told him anything else.

The next day, my mother accosted me on the back porch and called me an ugly name. I wasn't going to say anything, but something rose up in me, and I said, "You did it." That was the day our relationship as mother and daughter changed.

One Christmas Day I noticed my mother was bent over in the back of the trunk of her brother's car. I could see she had a cup in her hand. I don't remember her drinking until I was eighteen years old. I hated when she came home and had been drinking. She knew I didn't like it. She always wanted to play with me. I ignored her, and that made her mad. She would grab me—she was small but strong—and I would break loose from her. That made her mad. I would get mad and not speak to her for about three days.

Daddy didn't drink, and I did not want Mother to be a drinker. A good thing did come out of it. I have never swallowed any alcohol other than some real wine once during Communion in a church up north. I thought everybody used Welch's Grape Juice. Once it hit my throat, I knew it was real wine, or very old grape juice. I didn't like seeing my mother drunk and smelling alcohol on her breath when she went to sleep. So I never drank.

I went to a club one night, and a cousin came up to me and said, "Take a sip of this beer." I told him, "I don't drink." He replied, "You're going to drink this." I dumped the contents of the cup on him. Needless to say, he smelled like beer all night. I tried to tell him, but since he wouldn't listen, I had to show him. You are not going to make me do anything I don't want to do.

When I was twelve, a white man came to our house and asked my daddy if I could sit with his sickly mother. He would pay me. I believe Daddy knew him, or he would not have let me go with the man.

I still remember the car, a light green Ford. He drove to where a school now sits, drove up a hill, and told me to get out of the car. I asked, "Where are you taking me." He told me the house was just ahead. Now I was twelve, but I wasn't stupid. There was no road; we walked through the bushes. He stopped to relieve himself and then turned toward me, with his private parts showing. I began to cry. He quickly zipped his pants and shouted, "Get in the car!"

I believe he saw an angel because he never made a move toward me. He seemed to quickly change his mind. He drove me to about a mile from home and put me out of the car. He threatened to kill me if I told anyone what happened.

It was a cold winter day, and I had to walk the rest of the way home. By the time I got there, my feet were like a block of ice. I took off my shoes and placed my feet up against the woodstove. We were poor, and those shoes didn't have much sole on them.

Daddy was under a car; he was a mechanic. I believe I told him a lie, but I don't remember what it was. I was scared at first to tell him the truth. I thought he might hurt the man and go to jail. I did tell him about two weeks later. I don't know if Daddy ever spoke to that man.

I still see that man, and I'm not angry with him. I forgave him because I am so grateful he didn't go through with his plan. I believe he knows who I am, even though I am grown. One day I will walk up to him and tell him I forgive him.

His wife worked in a store in town. She was a nice lady. I often wondered if she knew she was married to a pedophile. I wondered how many little girls he touched or if I was his first experience. I believe he was an alcoholic because his face was always red.

Years later, I showed him to my husband and told him the story. You don't know how grateful I am to God that he did not allow anything to happen. He takes care of us when we don't even know him. God had a plan for my life.

My dad was no saint, but he was a good father. He and my mother shared the same sin as a lot of marriages do. Who can throw the first stone? We all have fallen short of the glory of God. We all have done things we're ashamed of.

Our dad made sure we had food to eat every day. He cooked for us at times. He laughed with us and hugged and kissed us. We felt love from our daddy.

Our mother was like a mother hen; if you messed with her children, she would fight. She didn't literally fight, of course, but when she got through cursing you out, you felt like you were in a fight for real. It didn't make any difference if we were in the wrong. She went to bat for us regardless. I would tell her, "Mom, that's not right." She would ask, "Charlene, who's the momma."

At church one Sunday when I was seventeen, my uncles came to me and said one in each family needed to go to college. They were teachers and advocates of getting an education. My mother and father never said anything to me about going to college. I was a senior in high school, and the school counselor never encouraged any of the black students to go to college.

This was the year of total integration. The counselor told the school's black students, including me, there was no need to go to college.

She refused to give us applications for scholarships. Black students would go in and ask for applications, and she would say she did not have anymore. Five minutes, later a white friend was sent in and ask for an application, and they would come out with one. Despite, the lack of encouragement to further our education the class of 1971 did very well. We have lawyers, doctors, teachers, social workers, preachers, plant managers, supervisors, nurses, a company vice president, and a CEO as alumni.

In the Evans family, there are thirty-eight degrees, with five pending now in universities. The thought was if one member of each of the twelve families went to college, siblings would follow. And that's what happened.

I was the second grandchild to graduate from A&T State University. My oldest cousin was the first grandchild to graduate from St. Augustine University. When we get together, we boast about which university has the most graduates in the family. My alma mater is the winner followed by North Carolina Central University and then St. Augustine University.

My college career started out at Kittrell Junior college. One day I was sitting in class and a classmate came and told me our house had burned down. I lived twenty minutes from the college. I said, "Stop playing," and he replied, "I'm for real." I ran out of class and went home.

When I got there, the house had burned to the ground. We lived two miles from the city limits, but only the rural fire department would respond, and they had to come twenty miles. When I got out of my car, my baby sister ran to me and said, "Charlene, this is all I got." She was in her pajamas. Tears ran down my cheek. I told her, "It's going to be all right." We moved in with our grandmother, who lived on the hill next to us. What we thought was bad was really a blessing. The house was old, and we had an outdoor toilet.

The churches in the area and people were so kind to us. They gave us money and clothing. When you go through a house fire, it's just like a death in the family. Everything that's dear to you is gone, all your pictures, your favorite dress, your dolls. It's a sad day. But I look at every house fire of people I know, and they always come out better. We were able to get a home loan and build a house with carpeting on the floor—no more cold floors—and a bathroom in the house. And there was running water. We were in heaven with four bedrooms.

We took new pictures and created new memories. It was wonderful. I was a sophomore in college at this time. My parents didn't have good credit, so they wondered how they would get furniture for the house. I took a job working third shift at a plant and paid for the furnishings. I bought bedroom sets for my parents and myself, twin beds for my brothers, a bed and dresser for my sisters, a kitchen set, and a living room set.

My grades were good; my first year I made the Dean's List. But after working third shift and not getting up for class, I started making more Cs. Sometimes I wished I had not taken the lead and taken the job to help my family because after that, everybody in the family looked to me. It was like I was in charge of the family, and I was just nineteen. That was too much responsibility to put on someone who had not turned twenty-one. I did not ask for it, nor did I want the responsibility. But it became my job to take care of the family.

I was always told I looked like my paternal grandmother and had the mouth of my maternal grandmother. She didn't play around. She said what she said and meant what she said. I was firm, just like she was. I admired her. I would drive her uptown, and she'd go into several high-priced stores. Clerks greeted her by her name and ask, "What can we get for you today?" I liked that white folks respected her. And because she paid her bill on time, she had good credit at those stores.

She bought a home and land on a fixed income. My parents lived from paycheck to paycheck. I knew I didn't want to live like that. I wanted to be like Grandma.

My husband came from a poor family, too. According to him, they were the poorest people in town. We were all poor in my circle. The first thing I told my husband was, "I'm not going to be poor like my parents." I was speaking into my own life. Sometimes you have to encourage yourself.

I saw what good credit could do for you, so I became a fanatic about paying my bills on time. I'm still like that and have a good credit rating as a result. I can buy what I want. The secret to that is that I buy within my means. Many people buy more than they can afford. Not me. I call it acting like you got it when you know you don't, and we know you don't. My degree in business administration afforded me the opportunity to know how to budget and stick to it. I taught my husband and my children how to budget.

When I graduated from A&T, I came home and told Daddy, "I can show you how to get out of debt." I took his bills and placed them in order, showing him what should be paid first and how much he should pay. He looked at me like I was crazy. I could tell he was thinking, *You are not going to tell me how to spend my money.*

Many people today want to get out of debt but won't do what it takes to achieve it. It's called discipline. And they are not going to let you tell them how to spend their money.

One time my Daddy and Momma were arguing, and my grandmother sided with her daughter, so I sided with Daddy. My grandma thought I was being disrespectful—and I was—so she put me out of her house. I didn't set foot in her house for two years.

One Christmas I decided to go to the family Christmas dinner. She was glad to see me, and I was glad to see her. Many years later, I talked with her about the Lord. She was so impressed. She said, "Gal, you're going to preach." "Grandma, you know I'm not going to be a preacher." Five years later, I gave my initial sermon. Grandma was prophesying and didn't know it.

I hate that my mother never got to see me preach; my father did. My mother did get to see me be a speaker for Women's Day services, but I was not a preacher at the time of her death. I wanted her to know God planted a seed in her womb, and she birthed a preacher.

When I was young, I had a recurring dream about soaring in the air. I would squat first and then leap into the air. I could feel the air against my face. It was the most wonderful feeling, such peace.

I always felt I would do great things. But being in the natural, I thought I would win a contest. I ordered the magazines and sent in my entry. I did that for years. I associated great things with money.

I heard Oprah say on her show that she had dreams in which she soared. Wait a minute. She had done great things in her lifetime, and that got my attention. Now that I was in the ministry, the great thing for me was telling people about the goodness of Jesus Christ and leading them into salvation. What can be better than that?

When Ulysses, my husband, and I were dating, we went to the county fair in our hometown. I just knew we would have a good time. He worked at one of the highest-paying plants in the area. He spent only twenty dollars, and ten of that twenty he lost when he tried to find the ball under the old three-cup switch-a-roo trick. I saw the real cup, but it was too quick for him. He was upset about losing ten dollars. We just walked around the rest of the night. I was glad we rode the rides before he lost everything.

We went to Atlantic City. He played the slot machine and lost eighteen dollars. He looked so sad. He continued to play, won twenty dollars, and didn't play anymore. I lost forty-eight and won fifty-seven before I stopped playing. We are both conservative with our money, but I call him a miser. We don't believe in wasting money.

Let me go back to the incident at the fair. I asked Ulysses the million-dollar question: "Do you have to give your money to your mother." He worked full time and lived at home. I had to know because I had made up in my mind not to get involved with a man whose umbilical cord was still attached to his mother. He was the only boy. When you marry a man and his allegiance is to his mother and not to you, you're not cleaving to one another as God commands us to do once we get married. The wife will struggle in that situation. Sometime the mothers-in-law will let the daughters-in-law know that she is number one.

The order is God first, your spouse second, and your children third. Any other way is out of order. It's sad when Christian mothers will not let go of their children. The sinner's mother hasn't gotten that far in the Bible. Women, if you see firsthand that he is still attached to his mother and she loves it, even though she knows he is married to you, you better think twice before you say I do.

When I was in eleventh grade, a white man killed a young black man for speaking to his daughter-in-law. The man was acquitted. The movie *Blood Done Sign My Name* tells that story. I could not believe someone could be killed for saying something, and the murderer go free. That really bothered me. I knew then I was a little militant in the sense I must stand for justice.

One Friday night there was a Christmas parade at six o'clock. I got there early to get a good place to stand because I was short. I was in the front row. The parade was moving right along, when a white school band passed, and a white cheerleader stretched out her arm and shook her pom-pom in my face. I believe she laughed. I couldn't believe it. I couldn't see, but I could feel all those little strings in my face. I believe she did it intentionally.

I grabbed the pom-pom because I was already mad that a black man had been killed in town. The cheerleader and I looked like we were sawing wood. She pulled it back and then I pulled it back. Mind you, the band was marching on, while she stood there, trying to get her pom-pom. Finally, I let it go, and she rejoined the band.

When I got to school that Monday, the principal called me in and told me I was expelled. I asked, "For what?" He replied, "Because of what you did at the parade." A teacher had told him what happened. I knew who the teacher was; I saw him that night, standing behind me.

I asked the principal, "How are you going to expel me from school when I had gone home, relaxed for about three hours, and then went to the parade. It was not a school parade; it was the town parade and it didn't have anything to do with school." Furthermore, I knew when I left school he had no authority over me. I guess he thought about it. He called me back into his office at the end of the day and withdrew the expulsion. I didn't tell my parents of that incident until later in life. I thought, *Why tell them? Nothing came of it.*

TESTIMONY

When I went into the ministry fifteen years ago, I began to ask God if there was sin in my life I personally needed to call out to Him and repent of. I waited for a response from God, and all of a sudden, this picture flashed in my mind. The image flashed in my head was from so many years ago, it had to be the Holy Spirit bringing it back to my memory. Immediately I asked God to forgive me and was very remorseful because I remembered it. Isaiah 43:25 (NIV) says, "I, even I am he who blots out your transgressions, for your own sake, and remembers your sins no more." I thank God for forgiveness today!

When you're not saved, you can do ugly things, and it won't bother you. But when you get saved and continue to do ugly things, the Holy Spirit will convict you of your wrongdoing. And if it still doesn't bother you after being convicted, your heart has become hardened.

When I was sixteen years old, two girls and I walked into a funeral home. A little girl lay in the casket. She may have been five years old. I didn't know her. One of the other girls started to laugh. She had a water head. Then the other girl started to laugh. I was scared of dead people, but I began to laugh, too. But you eventually reap what you sow!

Twenty years after that, I had my third child, a beautiful little girl. She died two days after her birth, and we didn't know why. We had bought so much for this baby before she was born. She swallowed some meconium (stool) before she was born; I will tell the story later. Well I went into a depression for five years, but nobody knew it. I kept up a good front, laughing on the outside but crying in the inside. I could not figure out why my baby died. I was saved and living a Christian life.

When the Holy Spirit brought the experience at the funeral home to my memory, I knew I was reaping what I had sown two decades before. You see, that was somebody's child in the coffin. Then I started thinking about one of the girls; her son almost beat her father to death. The girl who laughed first moved move away and came back home. I saw her at the grocery store and asked if she remembered that incident. She said she did, so I told her of my experience. I told her she needed to repent of that. What she said next blew me away. She said, "You know, I had a grandson die. He had a water head."

All three of us reaped from the seed we had sown. But I wondered, *Why was I punished the worst? I didn't start the laughing.* The Holy Spirit spoke in my spirit and said, *You knew better.* Of the three, I was the only one in church. Luke 12:47 (NIV) says, "That servant who knows his master's will and does not get ready or does not do what his master wants will be beaten with many blows." So those who know the Word of God and won't obey will be beaten with many stripes.

I knew better, and they did too. But because I was in church, a greater responsibility was on me. How many know we can't sit under the Word of God and do as we please? But I thank

God! He has given me such peace about my daughter's death because He forgave me and that sin is under the blood of Jesus. Therefore, there is now no condemnation for those who are in Christ Jesus (Romans 8:1 NIV).

What the Devil meant for bad God turned around for my good. I opened a door, and the Devil came in and took my daughter's life. And God allowed it to happen. You see, it took her death to get me in the ministry. Right then God began to break and humble me. I began to seek the Lord. That's why I'll praise Him as long as I live. I'll sing praises unto the Lord even on my dying bed. The Lord is good, and His mercy endures forever.

THE DEATH OF MY DAUGHTER

On January 9, 1990, at 4:25 a.m., I gave birth to a beautiful baby girl. Oh how I had hoped for a boy since I already had two girls. But when the doctor announced a girl, I smiled. At that moment, I really didn't care as long as the baby was healthy.

I was two weeks overdue, and the doctor said the baby had a bowel movement while I was carrying her and swallowed a little meconium. After the baby was checked out, the doctor stated everything seemed to be fine. I was not able to see her until 12:00 p.m. All this time, they had been observing her, which I did not know.

When the nurse brought her in, she said, "You know she swallowed some meconium." I said yes and that the doctor said he thought he got it all. She told me, "If the baby starts turning blue, call for assistance immediately." Not being alarmed, I said okay. I didn't think anything would happen to her. I picked her up and began stroking her body, checking to see if everything was where it was supposed to be.

I remember wondering, *Why am I doing this?* It seemed strange. I didn't do it with my other babies. I was weak and excited. Family and friends visited me in the hospital, and the florist brought flowers, balloons, and candy that had been sent to me.

I was really excited about Ulysses staying in the delivery room with me. Every time I asked him if he was going to stay, he told me no and to stop telling people he was. The way he said it made me laugh. Well when the time came, he stayed. I had asked him to stay with my other births, but he said no. This time was different.

Ulysses had never seen me in the last stages of delivery. When the pain worsened, I moaned and groaned a little louder. I hear women, especially young ones, say it didn't hurt. I guess not when you are deadened from your waist to your feet. You will never hear me say it didn't hurt. It did.

When I had a hard contraction, I told Ulysses to come over and rub the bottom of my back until the contraction eased. He didn't know how much it meant to me to have him there. I think he thought the doctor would ask him to leave once the baby started coming, but I knew he wouldn't. I guess you can say he may have felt trapped.

After it was over, I think he was glad to have been there to see her born and hear her cry. I looked at him, and he had such a pleased look on his face. He never left me that night; he stayed with me in the recovery room until the early morning. He had experienced life coming into existence, and I believe he was touched by it. He never told me this, but I could tell from his reactions.

The next evening, around 5:00 p.m., the doctor came in and said, "We have taken X-rays of your baby and can see some meconium in her lungs." He decided she needed to be in a neonatal care unit, which meant transferring her to another hospital. He assured me she would probably be fine, but the other hospital was better equipped to handle her problem.

Suddenly, I was afraid for the first time, but I didn't show it to anyone.

I went into the nursery to see her. I began to cry, and the nurses assured me she was going to be okay. When the Life Care attendants arrived, they worked on her for about an hour. The only thing I can remember is seeing her in an incubator, with needles and tubes on each side of her head with a little blue and white cap on her head. Again I was assured, by the attendants this time, she would be fine. This was around 7:00 p.m. Despite their assurances, I was concerned. My heart ached that she was being transferred to another hospital, and I would remain at this one. I cried, scared I might not see her again. My doctor knew I wanted to go to the hospital the next day. He said, "If your blood pressure is down, I will release you."

Ulysses spent the night with me, sitting up in a chair and trying not to worry. We called the hospital around 9:00 p.m. and talked with the nurse on her case. She could not tell us much at that time, because they were working on her. She did mention that while she was at hospital they fed her, and they should not have done that. And that she was a sick baby. We called again around 1:00 a.m. and talked with the doctor. He repeated what the nurse had told us; she was a sick baby. That's all he would say, not giving me any hope.

I thought, *Doctors always tell you the worst in any situation to cover themselves.* I began to get upset. To keep Ulysses from knowing, I walked down the hall. As I got near the nursery, I laid my head against the wall, and the tears just flowed. What I would have given at that moment to hear my baby cry again.

This was around 4:00 a.m., and the halls were empty. A nurse noticed me and escorted me back to my room. She said, "I will be back as soon as I finish my work." She told me she usually didn't work that side of the hospital floor. But she felt the Lord had placed her there that night for a reason, and she felt I was that reason. She said she was a born-again Christian and wanted to pray for me, my husband, and our baby. She prayed a beautiful prayer. It seemed as if it lasted ten minutes. And then she left.

Later that morning, I asked the nurse who came in my room the name of the black nurse who had worked the third shift. She said, "There is no black nurse on third shift." I told her, "A woman prayed for me last night." She just said, "I don't know who you are talking about." I can see now that God has always had angels around me, just as you have them around you. She was an angel God sent to comfort me in my hour of need.

On January 10, I was released from the hospital at 11 a.m. I was so eager to get to the other hospital that I wanted to walk out of the hospital. But you know the hospital policy; you have to go down in a wheelchair. The staff could not find a wheelchair for fifteen minutes. Right then I felt like donating a wheelchair to the hospital because I thought that was pitiful. We left one hospital and headed straight for another hospital. My sisters-in-laws and mother-in-law went with us.

I couldn't wait to see my baby and see for myself if she was as sick as the nurse and doctor had stated. First we had to wash up and put on sterile gowns. When Ulysses and I walked in, there our baby lay, naked under a heat lamp and with two tubes in her mouth. A needle was on the right and left sides of her head. A tube ran from her navel. Another needle was in her right wrist drawing out blood and returning it to her body. Patches were all over her body. And she had been given a drug to paralyze her. It broke my heart to see her this way.

I wanted to scream but knew I could not because of the other sick babies in the room. So I just cried softly. I noticed a tear had run down her face and wondered if she was in pain. It broke my heart. The nurse was nice. She said, "You do have a sick baby, but she's not as sick as she looks. There at last was the little glimmer of hope I had been waiting for.

The doctor came in and said test showed she swallowed a little meconium, and it was in her lungs. They also found she had a hole in her heart. He said that was not uncommon and usually closed as the baby grows.

I began to feel better, though I could hardly stand up straight because of the stitches from giving birth. And I was weak. My baby was on a respirator. This was a Wednesday, and the doctor felt sure she would be off by Saturday. She was sick but doing well.

After a couple of hours visiting with her, we headed home, feeling good about her recovery. Around 5:30 a.m. the telephone rang, and I shouted for Ulysses to answer it. It was the doctor. Our baby had experienced a setback, but they thought she was stable now. Again at 6:45 a.m. the telephone rang again. I picked it up on the first ring. The doctor said we needed to get to the hospital right away. I asked if she was all right. Again he said, "You need to get here as soon as possible." Ulysses called his sisters, Marie and Willie Mae and they took off work to go with us.

When we arrived at the hospital, I said, "I am afraid to go up" because I expected the worst. Ulysses let us off at the door and went to park the car. He told us not to wait for him; he was afraid, too. Marie waited for him, and Willie Mae went up with me and our daughters, Shelby and Stephanie.

I recognized one of the nurses in the hallway and ran up to her. I immediately asked, "Is she all right?" She said, "Let me get the doctor." As she turned, I grabbed her arm and asked, "Is she dead?" She quietly said, "I'm sorry." I screamed!

Some doctors and nurses were having a meeting in an open conference room. I broke up that meeting, screaming and crying.

My mind was racing. I thought, *This cannot be happening.* Willie Mae tried to calm me down, but it didn't work. I remember beating the table where the doctors and nurses sat. I looked around and saw Stephanie watching me and crying. Shelby must have been standing behind me because I didn't see her. I was glad my sisters-in-law were with us because Ulysses and I were in total shock. I had never experienced death in my immediate family, but Ulysses had lost a sister and his father.

Everyone was watching me. I knew then I needed to calm down because I was scaring the children. They ushered us into a consulting room to try and explain her death to us. I ask the doctor, "What happened?" He shook his head and said, with tears in his eyes, "We just don't know." I thought I was listening to the doctor, but my mind was racing. They could not explain her death. The head doctor said, "We are just as shock as you are, and honestly, we don't know what happened. She was doing fine and then all of a sudden, something happened. What that was we do not know."

He tried to encourage me to let them do an autopsy. I quickly said no! I was so filled with anger at that moment. I thought, *How dare you ask me to let you cut her up and put her back together. She is a baby.* Another doctor admitted the autopsy might not reveal anything. I knew for sure then I was not going to let them explore on her. I could tell Ulysses wanted to do the autopsy because he kept saying he wanted to know why she died. I told him at that time it must have been the Lord's will, what else could I say.

They asked us if we wanted to see and hold the baby. I had never touched a dead person, but this was different. This was my daughter, so I said yes.

They brought Sherrell in to me, dressed in a red and white dress with matching panties and wrapped in a blanket. I reached out my arms, took her, and held her soft body next to mine. I kissed her several times. We all cried together and I rubbed her face, her legs and arms. But Shelby would not even look at her. She was afraid, and her head was under a jacket that she had on. We didn't make her.

We kept our baby in that room for about forty-five minutes. I was afraid in the beginning, but Lord knows I was grateful for that time with her. It was the second time I got to hold her. They took pictures of her and baptized her. We were given other tokens, such as her footprints and the cap she wore to the hospital.

On the way home it was completely silent. Then out of the blue, I asked, "Do you think the doctors did something wrong." I don't know who responded, but I heard, "I don't know." The doctors were shocked about her death, and that made me wonder for an instant. The doctor had said she would probably come off the respirator on Saturday, but instead, we were burying her Saturday.

When we returned home, my mother and sisters were waiting for us. I walked into the kitchen and found my mother at the refrigerator. She looked afraid, like she didn't know what to say to me. I said, "Ma, she's dead." "I know." My Mother and Sylvia and Dale followed me into the bedroom, and we all cried as a family.

By this time I was so disoriented I couldn't think straight. This lasted for about three months. I couldn't read, I couldn't pray, and I couldn't sleep. I did not understand why this happened. I was saved and had a baby with my husband. Ulysses and I could not get over how kind family and friends were to us. He kept saying, "Everybody is so nice."

The telephone didn't stop ringing until after the funeral. You do get tired of repeating the story over and over, but you're grateful for the calls. They show people are concerned about what you're going through. My mother-in-law stayed with us for two weeks after the funeral. Every day she took three or four cards out of the mailbox. She said, "People sure are thinking about you." For the moment, that made me feel good. I realized Ulysses and I had been kind to people, and the calls and cards we continued to receive were proof of this.

One thing I learned from my daughter's death is the best thing to say is you're sorry for their loss and ask if there's anything you can do. Leave it at that. Don't try to rationalize why the person died, because you don't know the answer to that. I had people say some crazy things to me, but they meant well. They said, "The Lord saw a need to take your little angel," or, "God needed another angel in heaven." God has millions of angels; why would He need her? And this one: "You should find comfort in knowing your child is in heaven." I would one day but not two days after she was born.

One lady told me, "You still have two girls." Yes I do, but I wanted that baby, too. Or, "Be glad it wasn't a boy; it was another girl." I still wanted her. I planned for her. When these things are first said, they bring some comfort. But we're not really conscious of what is being said. Later, after the funeral and you're sitting alone, it comes back to you.

I said to a preacher, "I know God doesn't make mistakes." His response was, "He's not supposed to." Why couldn't he just say, "No, He doesn't"? That would have made me feel good, coming from someone who knows the Word of God. When you're mourning the loss of someone you love, you're really looking for someone to share comforting words not their opinion.

When a baby dies, there is usually a graveside funeral. I said, "If inactive members can have a funeral knowing they never come to church, my baby can have a funeral, too." I remember walking down the aisle in the church and seeing her in that small casket. I cried out, "My baby!" I was told the church was full and some people had to stand. I didn't know that.

My daddy came by the day after the funeral and said all the wrong things. He said my stepmother told him to come by and see how I was doing. Did somebody really need to tell him his daughter needed him? Then he said the church was full because of him, my mother-in-law, and me and Ulysses—in that order. What? I was really insulted. I lost a child, but they came for him. What did he lose? I looked at my daddy and thought, *That's pitiful. You don't get it I'm hurting. It's not about you this time.*

The rest of my family and Ulysses' family and our friends were wonderful. My mother was really there for me. My sisters-in-law and a cousin Margaret kept the house going.

After the funeral I began to grieve Sherrell's death. I was in shock in the beginning so I guess I was in denial. Three months later, I was waiting for someone to wake me from a bad dream. Then I began to go in and out of depression. I had to visit her grave to get some relief.

I was angry I guess that was part of the grief process. I remembered all those remarks about God wanting her. I told Marie I was angry. She asked, "Charlene, who are you angry with?" I quickly said, "God." She told me I shouldn't be angry with Him, I shot back, "You don't understand how I feel. You haven't lost anyone dear to you."

I believe people think you commit blasphemy when you say you're angry at God. You have to know that God knows what you're thinking. He can read your mind. He's not going to forsake you because you're mad at Him. He knows your pain and understands your feelings at that moment. God is not like us. He doesn't stop loving us because we say something that's not nice.

I feel like there is nothing worse that can happen to me in my life, for I have carried a baby for nine months and she lived two days.

There is no other trial and tribulation that can compare to losing a child. Two months later, I was watching the news and heard a report that another baby had died in the same hospital. I was glued to the television. It also was a black baby.

I started wondering, *Can this be a conspiracy?* When doctors don't know why your baby died, you look for reasons. At first they didn't know the reason for the other baby's death. This young mother allowed them to do an autopsy. It showed the baby was given too much potassium. The needle the nurse used to give the injection was too large.

So I prayed and asked the Lord to direct me as to what to do. When my doctor called to check on me his office sent flowers, I asked him if he heard about the baby on the news who died at the hospital. He said yes. So I asked the question about the potassium. He told me if you're given too much potassium, you will die.

I hung up the telephone and went and got my hospital bill. Guess what? The last thing my daughter got on the day she died was an injection of potassium. I don't have to tell you what my first thought were. *Did they give her too much potassium with the same large needle?* My mind started racing. *What if the nurse intentionally did it?*

I contacted a lawyer. He retrieved the medical records for me. He read them and then sent them to me, and I read them. I worked at a hospital, so I was used to reading doctors' and nurses' handwriting and understood the medical terminology. The lawyer informed me that since I refused to have an autopsy, there was no way to prove if she got too much potassium. Can you imagine having to live with that question for the rest of your life?

So I was thinking, *Maybe they accidentally killed her,* or, *Did they do it on purpose?* Whatever happened to her, I realized I would never have the answer to the question of what happened to my baby. I had to face the fact she was dead. She was gone, and I had to deal with my grief and move on. This was easier said than done.

I started thinking about everything I did while carrying her, wondering if there was something I could have done to prevent this from happening. This was the guilt stage. My daughter Stephanie told me it was my fault because I ran up and down the steps. And I did do that to try and make the baby drop. She wanted a sister so badly, somebody to look up to her, and she took the baby's death really hard.

Once I accepted the fact our baby was dead and worked through the stages of grief, I began to heal. It took me five years to heal because of the depression. I just asked God to strengthen me.

One day I was having a bad day, and I just hollered out, "God help me!" at the top of my voice. Instantly, the depression left me. I felt a weight lift from me, and I have never again grieved her death. God gave me such peace about her death.

Shelby came and hugged me and asked, "Momma, you all right?" Ulysses and Stephanie stayed in the den and never checked on me. I think they thought I was about to lose it. And I'm here to tell you, I was. I was close to a nervous breakdown. That's why I praise God the way I do. I know He kept my mind. I know He did.

When I go to the church where she is buried, I rarely visit her grave. She's not there. She's in heaven, waiting for me to get there. I have grown from that experience. When something like this happens to you, it's like your eyes open, and you view things much differently.

I used to read the Bible, but I started to study the Bible. I know now there's a difference between reading and studying. I thought about how Jesus suffered and figured it must be a part of living. So there are times in life when we have to suffer losses.

I hate to think where I would be if I had not been in church. When something like this happens in your life, it will set you back if you're weak. And that's what the Devil wants to happen. But I didn't give in to the pressure. The Lord strengthened me for the test. That's what I see it as, a test from the Lord.

I learned how to comfort others who have lost a child. I wrote this story about my baby November 16, 1990, ten months after her death. It was the best therapy for me, putting it down on paper and sharing it, letting other people know how I felt. To God be the glory!

Picture of the baby casket and flowers

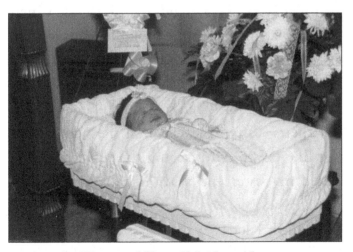

Picture of Sherrell in the casket.
Sherrell was born January 9, 1990.
Sherrell died January 11, 1990.
Sherrell was buried January 13, 1990.

MY BROTHER DENNIS

My sister always said we had a half-brother, but I never paid any attention to her. One day Dale called me and said, "Go get the newspaper." I asked, "Who's in it? She replied, "Your brother."

I went to the store and got the paper. When I looked at his picture, I thought, *He looks just like our daddy. He has a nose just like ours and a good grade of hair curly like our daddy.* You see, God has a sense of humor when some men say a child is not theirs. Often the children they deny look just like them. After seeing the resemblance, I called my sister and said, "I believe he is our brother."

I think I let two days pass and then called him on his job and told him I wanted to come and see him and that I was his sister. It was like one of the talk show episode when you meet a sibling for the first time. I walked into his office and greeted him. Then I just stared at him. He appeared to be in his thirties. Finally I said, "Excuse me, but you look just like my daddy." I told him I saw his picture in the newspaper.

We started talking. He said he always knew who his father was, and because I acknowledged that he was our brother, a void in his life was filled. I shared things with him about the family. I told him I hated he missed my sister Nita's funeral. He said, "I didn't miss it. I was there at the wake." I was so glad to hear that.

Our daddy was a mechanic, and Dennis works on his cars. I told him our daddy loved a Dr. Pepper. He had a soda machine outside the house, and no matter what button you hit, that soda came out. He bought Dr. Pepper because he knew we didn't like it, but we all ended up drinking them. I really didn't like it; I thought it tasted like medicine. Dennis said that was his favorite drink. I laughed. Guess what? It's now my favorite soda. It no longer tastes like medicine to me.

Our father was in a rest home at that time. I took Dennis there and asked my father, "Is this your son?" He nodded, smiled, and said yes. We didn't care about the circumstances of his birth. We shared the same blood. So for the last year and a half of our daddy's life, he got to know Dennis and his family.

I took Dennis to our home church to introduce him to his family. Some family members were upset with me, but that was all right. I was not going to sweep this under the rug.

We have been a family ever since I walked into his office. My siblings and I accept him, and we love him, his wife, and his children. He attends the family reunion, and we have family dinners at each other's home.

BETRAYAL

Webster's Dictionary says "betrayal" means, "to be a traitor to or to commit treason against; to be unfaithful or disloyal."

When you do everything you can for a person or persons, and they turn around and betray you, that hurts. Anytime a person betrays you, there seems to be envy, jealousy, and bitterness in his or her heart.

There also seems to be a bit of resentment toward others in the person's heart. It can be repressed for years, but once the individual notice how God continues to bless others and not him or her, resentment begins to surface. That Serpent's spirit comes to the forefront, and the lies begin. This is why the Bible tells us in Psalm 118:8 (NIV), "It is better to take refuge in the Lord than to trust in man." We don't believe that, but Jesus will never hurt us the way family and friends will or have. He's the best friend you will ever have.

I heard Bishop Jakes say, "You will have to be strong to be successful because you will have haters. Whatever you're doing to make them hate you, do it some more. Are you able to handle the pressure that goes with success? Successful people are envied and disliked because of their success. People want what you got, but they don't want to do, what you did to get it."

If Christians try to live a righteous life, help people in need, and give God what belongs to Him (the tithes), God's favor will be on their lives. Why are people so upset with those doing it God's way, when they see the favor of God on their lives, and that God enlarges their territories when we all can do it God's way?

It's the choices we make in life. I see people with every new phone that comes out, yet they live from paycheck to paycheck. And when I pull out my flip phone, they laugh. I laugh, too, because I don't have a bill. My daughter Shelby gave me mines for Christmas because

I wouldn't get one. She put me on her plan. Who's laughing now?

Luke 21:16–18 (NIV) says, "You will be betrayed even by parents, brothers, relatives and friends, and they will put some of you to death. All men will hate you because of me "Jesus". But not a hair of your head will perish."

Willie Lynch gave a speech in 1712, describing how to keep blacks separated. It's sad to say some blacks are still living in that era. We have been freed, but some are still in bondage to the past of envy, jealousy, and distrust.

This speech was said to have been delivered by Lynch on the bank of the James River in Virginia. He was a British slave owner in the West Indies. He was invited to Virginia to teach his methods to slave owners there. He claimed his method was foolproof. Lynch stated that if it were installed correctly, it would control the slaves for at least three hundred years. According to Lynch, his method was so simple any member of the family and the overseer could use it. He assured them his method worked on his plantation and would work in the South.

Lynch experimented with young and old slaves. He outlined a number of differences between the slaves and took those differences and made them bigger. He looked at their age, color, intelligence, size, sex, plantation sizes, status on the plantations, the owner's attitudes, whether they had fine or coarse hair and if they were short or tall. He said he used fear, distrust, and envy for control purposes.

Lynch told the Virginia slave owners distrust was stronger than trust and envy stronger than adulation, respect, or admiration. He stated that after slaves received this indoctrination, the control would continue and become self-fueling and self-generating for hundreds of years.

The slave owners were told to put the old black male against the young black male and vice versa. According to Lynch, "You must put the dark skin slaves against the light skin slaves and vice versa. You must put the black female slaves against the black male slaves and vice versa. You must have white servants and overseers (who) distrust all Blacks."

But it was also necessary the slaves trust and depend on the owners. They had to love, respect, and trust only them. He stated these were the keys to controlling slaves. He told them to use his methods, to have their wives and children use them, and never miss an opportunity to use his techniques. If used intensely for a year, the slaves will remain perpetually distrustful of each other.

My brothers and sisters, can we rise above what was done to us hundreds of years ago? Get rid of the envy and jealousy, and be happy for your brothers and sisters who are excelling in life.

THE CHURCH

Church folks, church folks, church folks! I have heard all my life that some church folks have mean spirits. Let me tell you this is true. I am not a doormat people can walk all over. I stand up for myself and for others. The Bible tells us to speak for the ones who cannot speak for themselves.

As a pastor, you get to see the good, the bad, the mean, the oppositional, the stubborn, the self-righteous, and the powerful ones in church. Oh yes, there are some power holders in the church; it has to be done their way, or your tenure as a pastor will not be heavenly.

If you were to ask those running the churches to teach a Sunday school lesson, I believe you would find many of them cannot. But church members will go to them for direction and instruction instead of to their leader. It's because they have held positions in the churches for too many years and they refuse to relinquish the authority to the pastor, who is head of the flock.

Pastoring is not hard if there's an anointing to do it. It's the sheep that makes pastoring so difficult. You have to deal with more negative than positive attitudes. You have competitive ministers, always trying to show you they know more than you do. I always wonder, *Where is their church.* Maybe God has not called them to pastor but, instead, to humble themselves and help their leader to build up the kingdom of God.

It's the strangest thing. Women are often the worst critics of other women in the ministry. There are pastors who are not keen on the idea of women preachers, but they are cordial and respectful. Women sometimes try to make you feel bad. I can be standing with a couple of male pastors and a woman will walk up and greet them as pastors. But then she looks at me, smiles, and says, "Hey Charlene," knowing I'm also a pastor. That's what I call a mean spirit.

If I go to my family reunion, I'm just another cousin. But if I am invited to your church to preach, I believe you should honor the position God has placed me in. When you were in school, you didn't call the principal by his or her first name. You didn't call the secretary or librarian by their first names. You didn't call the teachers by his or her first names. You didn't call the coaches by their first names. You didn't call the janitor or cafeteria personnel by their first names. That would have been disrespectful. So why is it so easy to disrespect God's servants? We know the Devil hates us, but what did we do to you? The world is turned upside down when it comes to things of God. Did I mention that I'm talking about people who confess to being Christians?

One of my dearest friends is a preacher and she can be standing right beside her husband, who is a pastor, and people will greet him as pastor and look toward her and greet her by her name. Knowing they both are preachers of the gospel, this represents a mean spirit. I have had people call me by my first name in the pulpit. One went as far as to say Mrs. Morton. Some women will sneer at you when they do it. Believe me they know what they're doing.

And I don't believe the pastors who say it doesn't bother them to be called by their first names. Let that preacher get in a room with a lot of dignitaries or preachers, and they will pull out every degree and title they have. Sometime it's your title or position that speaks to your gifting.

This is for all the women who have never picked up the Bible to see what it says about women preachers: you need to repent for all the hurtful things you have said and done to your sister in the ministry. Read the Bible for yourself, so you can stop being critical of your sisters who serves God and has answered the call to pastor. How about lifting up a sister instead of tearing one down?

We know Miriam and Deborah were prophets. What is a prophet? A prophet is a preacher, one who speaks on God's behalf about the present or speaks to the future.

On the day of Pentecost, 120 men and women were praying in the temple in Jerusalem. According to Acts 2, the Holy Spirit fell on this group of individuals not just on the disciples. The believers were among thousands of people who made this trip to Jerusalem from every part of the Mediterranean world.

These 120 men and women were filled with the Holy Spirit and moved out into the crowd. They spoke a language they didn't understand, but the people understood what they were saying. That's why some in the crowd hollered out, "You're all drunk!"

Peter had to stand and explain what was happening. Because the women were preaching and declaring the words of God, Peter had to remind the crowd what Joel had said would happen: "In the last days, God says, I will pour out my Spirit on all people. Your sons and daughters will prophesy, your young men will see visions, your old men will dream dreams. Even on my servants, both men and women, I will pour out my Spirit in those days and they will prophesy." Acts 2:17-18 (NIV). The Holy Spirit was being poured out on sons and daughters and on male and female servants. This was not only a blessing for women but for people of all races and classes.

First Timothy 2:12 (NIV) says, "I do not permit a women to teach or to have authority over a man; she must be silent." If this statement is the absolute truth forever and for every people, we have to apply it in every area of our lives. There are absolute truths in Scripture, and there are truths relative to a given time and situation. If this Scripture is true, the women running churches need to sit down. It's not just the deacons and pastors; we have women running churches.

This means you can't teach, you can't be the clerk, you can't be the superintendent, and you can't sing in the choir. You would be talking, and you're supposed to be quiet in church. I think you get the point I am trying to make.

Where would the church be today without women in the church? There would be no church because most of the men would be home. I believe most women get saved before their husbands, and that's the reason the men are in church. We pray them in.

Men in leadership should repent for hurting women in leadership positions and hindering them from operating in the gifting God has placed in them. I look at churches pastored by men who oppose women in the ministry.

There's a great struggle in those churches. Membership is low, the money is low, and the Holy Spirit is nowhere to be found.

How can God bless the ministries of these male pastors when they are against what He is doing in women, in the ministries He's raising up? Should we listen to men and sit on our gifts, or should we listen to God and step out of the box? I believe God is looking for willing vessels—male or female—to serve Him. I tell people when I get to heaven I don't think God will be upset with me for sharing the gospel with people and leading them into salvation.

Let me ask a question. Did you know 886 verses of Scripture come to us from women? I didn't, but I know now because of studying and reading the Bible and other resources and not taking the word of someone else.

This is why preachers tell you to read the Bible for yourself. Don't take our word; you need to make sure we are right. This has caused a lot of confusion with women preachers. Ladies, you have taken the word of a man who has interpreted the Scripture wrong. Read the Bible!

Phillip had five daughters, and they were all evangelists; they were preachers. We know Deborah was a prophet, and the leader Barak wouldn't move unless she went first. Miriam was a prophet and there were other women.

Paul told Timothy all Scripture was given by God for teaching. If God really did prohibit women from teaching, men should not read the verses that came from a woman, such as Mary in Luke 1:46–55 (NIV).

And Mary said: My soul glorifies in the Lord and my spirit rejoices in God my Savior, for he has been mindful of the humble state of his servant. From now on all generations will call me blessed, for the Mighty One has done great things for me, holy is his name. His mercy extends to those who fear him, from generation to generation. He has performed mighty deeds with his arm; he has scattered those who are proud in their inmost thoughts. He has brought down rulers from their thrones but has lifted up the humble. He has filled the hungry with good things but has sent the rich away empty. He has helped his servant Israel, remembering to be merciful to Abraham and his descendants forever, even as he said to our fathers.

I guess no male preacher has ever taught or preached on these Scriptures written by a woman. All Scripture was given by God for teaching the believers.

Priscilla and Aquila took Apollo's aside and taught him. If you read the Scripture, you will find Priscilla's name is mentioned first three times when talking about the couple. They had a church in their home. Their ministry was probably one of pastor and co-pastor. It's possible she may have been the leader in their church ministry.

Mary and Priscilla were not the only women colleagues Paul mentioned. Of the thirty-nine coworkers he mentioned by name, more than one-fourth was women.

The comment that gets me is, "The Bible says 'men.'" Do you not know that is the term for the whole human race? If that were true, we couldn't be saved, because the Bible says all men might be saved. That leaves out women and children. God is a God of love. He would not leave us out. He sent Jesus to save all of us.

We know Mary Magdalene and other women were the first to tell the good news about the resurrection of Jesus Christ. Women went to the tomb, found it empty, and ran to tell the other disciples. Jesus could have showed up where the disciples were hiding out. But He allowed a woman to get the message first. I guess that old saying is true. There are three ways of communication: telegraph, telephone, and tell a woman. Some didn't believe Mary Magdalene when she told the truth then, and some still don't believe today when women speak the truth.

Do you remember when we used to go to church and men had a Sunday school class taught by men, and women had a Sunday school class taught by women. And the children had a class? In Paul's days, men were probably on one side in the church service and women on the other side, just as we had seen in our churches.

Years ago, revelation came, and men's and women's classes were combined. Women began teaching men, as well as men teaching women. When we get married, we are to become one. But when we went to church, we were separated one from each other. It's so good to look out and see husbands and wives sitting together in the congregation.

Pertaining to women being quiet in the church, were they causing confusion and disruption during the church services? Paul was telling them to be quiet and to ask their husbands questions at home if they didn't understand what was said. You see, they were probably hollering across the aisles to ask their husbands questions. Some were probably just learning to read and didn't understand what was being said. It's possible they disagreed with what was being said and they were trying to teach their doctrines. Or they may have been refusing to give up their ways of worshipping.

Some say the women could have been speaking in tongues. No preacher wants someone else talking while he or she is preaching. It's a distraction from the Word of God. So you see, the women needed to be quiet at that time.

We have to remember that was their culture and not ours. Many things are done in Eastern culture today that we don't do in our Western culture. So why do we have to adhere to that one particular thing.

First Timothy 2:8 (NIV) says, "I want men everywhere to lift up holy hands in prayer, without anger or disputing." We don't see much of this in our churches. Men, if you take the Bible to be literal about everything, you should step up to the plate and lift your hands when you pray. But you've probably got too much pride for that. Can I get an Amen, women?

What then shall we say, brothers? When you come together, everyone has a hymn, or a word of instruction, a revelation, a tongue or interpretation. All of these must be done for the strengthening of the church. If anyone speaks in a tongue, two, or at the most three should speak, one at a time, and someone must interpret. If there is no interpreter, *the speaker should keep quiet in the church;* and speak to himself, and God. (1 Corinthians 14:26–28 NIV, emphasis added)

Two or three prophets should speak, and the others should weigh carefully what is said. And if a revelation comes to someone who is sitting down, the first speaker should stop "*hold his peace.*" For you can all prophesy in turn so that everyone may be instructed and encouraged? The spirits of the prophets are subject to the control of the prophets. (1 Corinthians 14:29–32 NIV, emphasis added)

Paul tells those speaking in tongues they should be quiet. He tells the prophets they should stop talking when another began to speak. And he told the women to be quiet. Paul was setting order in the church services. But people have singled out women to be quiet when, in fact, he told others disrupting the service to be quiet.

For God is not a God of disorder but of peace. (1 Corinthians 14:33 NIV)

These gifts are regulated not by God but by the church. Paul stated God was a "God of order and peace."

Therefore, my brothers, be eager to prophesy "we certainly don't see this in the churches" and do not forbid speaking in tongues. But everything should be done in a fitting and orderly way. (1 Corinthians 14:39 NIV)

We see in the Scripture he did not forbid speaking in tongues. It just needed to be spoken in order.

First Timothy is one of three pastoral letters written by Paul to instruct the next generation of church leaders. Paul tells us the purpose of the letter in 1Timothy 3:14-15 (NIV): "Although I hope to come to you soon, I am writing you these instructions so that, if I am delayed, you will know how people ought to conduct themselves in God's household."

Throughout this letter Paul not only describes appropriate conduct for Timothy but also how believers are to conduct themselves. Could it be Paul was stating his opinion as to how the church should function? But some in the churches have read it as a command from God.

Church folks, church folks, church folks! I have endured more hurt from church folks than anyone else, which includes my family. But I can see the "fruits of the Spirit" in my life. I have the love of Jesus in my heart, put there by the Holy Spirit. The joy of the Lord is truly my strength, and I could not have made it as a pastor without it. I am amazed at the peace I have, which I do not understand. I'm able to overlook the critics. I have always been a person who loves to treat people the way I want to be treated—gentle, kind, and good to them. I am faithful to the call on my life. I can tell you that God humbled me; I did not humble myself. Now I know how to stay humble through prayer, which is meekness.

Well I have not hit anyone or cursed anyone, even though my blood pressure has been up many times. So I guess you can say I am enduring the trials of life. That's temperance. But some church folk are just mean. I think I may slip up with this fruit because people bait you, provoke you, and challenge you constantly. I will not do it, because the Holy Spirit is keeping me, and convicting me of my wrong thoughts.

Galatians 5:25 (NIV) says, "Since we live by the Spirit, let us keep in step with the Spirit." This is my goal in life. If I had to start a church all over, I would never do it in my hometown. Jesus was not accepted in His hometown. What made me think I would be accepted? I guess thinking it had been 2,000 years since Jesus was rejected, and we are being taught the Word of God and receiving new revelations.

Maybe, just maybe, it wouldn't be like that now. I now see why the majority of pastors in my hometown are from another city. It's better if people don't know you. The hurt I experienced from some of my family members, was a lack of support, critical spirits, and disrespect for the position God placed me in.

Even the ones who knew me before I became a pastor always challenged me and resisted the instructions I gave them as their leader. Paul told Timothy, "All Scripture is God breathed and is useful for teaching, rebuking, correcting and training in righteousness, so that the man of God may be thoroughly equipped for every good work" (2 Timothy 3:16–17 NIV).

Many people don't function in the gifts of the Holy Spirit, which He gave them through the church. They are too concerned about what other people think. They do not think about how God wants to use them. Can you take a bold step of faith for the Lord and not worry about what others think?

The church needs to honor the gifts of the Holy Spirit in all its members. To do so creates an atmosphere where people feel comfortable operating in their gifts and without being criticized and dishonored by others. The Spirit of God is so often quenched in churches because of the critical stares and the fact they are not able to recognize the power flowing through their members.

Matthew 13:57 (NIV) says, "And they took offense at him. But Jesus said to them, only in his hometown, and in his own house is a prophet without honor." The people of Nazareth were so familiar with Jesus and His family that they refuse to be instructed by Him. That stumbling block caused them to dishonor Jesus. Mark 6:4–5 (NIV) reads, *"He could not do any miracles* there, except lay his hands on a few sick people and healed them (emphasis added).

Jesus was amazed at the lack of their faith. The most anointed man in town was among them, but because they knew who His parents were, who His grandparents, brothers, and sisters were, not one miracle was performed.

There's a lot of sickness in the body of Christ "church" because there is no honor for the man or woman of God operating in his or her gifting in those churches. When we honor the man or woman of God in our heart, God's power is made available to heal. Do you let the fact that you know your pastor or leader personally keep you from honoring the gifts the Holy Spirit wants to manifest through that individual?

Sadly, things have not changed that much since Jesus' time. We know the Pharisees and the Sadducees were religious in keeping the Law. And they went against Jesus in His ministry of help. Preachers are attacked today by that same religious spirit. Instead of being religious, believers should have Jesus in their hearts for others to see by doing what Jesus did.

LEADERSHIP

Ibelieve leaders are born with the ability to handle certain situations and confront problems head-on. As a youth, people often told me, "Charlene, you're a good girl." When you hear that repeatedly, you begin to believe it. And that's what happened to me.

I started carrying myself in a way that was pleasing to people because I liked hearing them say that about me. I didn't smoke or drink; good girls didn't do that. I did try smoking a Camel cigarette without a filter. It left a bad taste in my mouth, and that's probably why I don't smoke; it was awful. I thank God today for my healthy lungs.

I can look back and see God guiding my steps from my youth into adulthood. Every job I ever had was preparing me for ministry. I worked with the mentally ill and the court system, where I learned to have compassion for people. I worked with a company that built houses. That gave me knowledge of building. I drew the building plans for our church on a plain sheet of paper. I was told I needed an engineer before I could get the plans drawn up. Not so. The architect used what I had drawn on the paper.

I opened a restaurant to learn how to deal with the public. I had a day care to learn how to love children. I taught Sunday school for many years and started a home Bible study group, which lasted for two years. And then I went into the ministry. The Lord orders our steps. Hallelujah!

Paul was not against women preachers, women teachers, or women church leaders. In fact, Paul was very supportive of women in the ministry, as the Scriptures states. Why would Paul ask the church in Rome to receive the woman minister Phoebe with all due honor and then turn around and contradict himself, telling Timothy never to allow women as church leaders?

Paul was dealing with an ungodly woman leader and letting Timothy know what it meant to be a godly leader—both for men and women. First Timothy 3:1 (NIV) says, "Here is trustworthy saying: If anyone sets his "or her" heart on being an overseer, he "or she" desires a noble task." When talking about leaders Paul said anyone that meant male or female. If that were not true, he would have made it plain for us.

First Timothy 3:11 (NIV) says, "In the same way, their wives are to be women worthy of respect, not malicious talkers but temperate and trustworthy in everything." In *The Amplified Bible* it reads, "The women likewise must be worthy of respect and serious, not gossipers, but temperate and self-controlled, "thoroughly" trustworthy in all things."

When Paul spoke of women with leadership responsibilities, he used the word "likewise," which is the same as saying "in the same way" women are to be serious and faithful in all things. Therefore, Paul treated men and women the same, as coworkers in the gospel. He was absolutely committed to equality.

Paul was talking about men serving as deacons in 1Timothy 3:8-10. Deacons likewise, are to be men worthy of respect, sincere, not indulging in much wine, and not pursuing dishonest gains. They must keep hold of the deep truth of the faith with a clear conscious. They must first be tested and then if there is nothing against them, let them serves as deacons. He went on to say in v.11, "In the same way their wives are to be women worthy of respect, not malicious talkers but temperate and trustworthy in everything." Paul did not come out against all women because of the mistakes of one.

Because one woman was outspoken, that is not a reason to ban all women from public ministry. In 1Timothy 3:11, Paul stated the necessary qualities for godly women to be released into public ministry. Every one of us should follow God's leading into whatever ministry He chooses. This is true for men and women.

Here are two short stories to explain why I believe leaders are born. One day Shelby called me and said her husband was being arrested. When I asked why, she said when he went to register his gun they ran a check on his name. The officer told him there was a warrant for his arrest. Well we knew that was a mistake, and I told her I would call the sheriff because I knew him. He knew me very well. I had been in meetings with him, and we were in school together.

I called and told the sheriff, "You have the wrong man." I told him the Roy Hunt he had in custody was my son-in-law. I told the sheriff where he worked and lived, and that he was a college graduate with a degree in engineering. And that he was a deacon in the church. The sheriff checked out the information I gave him and found it to be true. Roy was released in fifteen minutes. Leaders do what needs to be done without having a meeting. Leaders are born!

This same sheriff also saved my daddy's house. My brother got into some trouble and was put in jail. My daddy got him out of jail by putting his house up as bail collateral.

Several months later, the sheriff called and told me my daddy was going to lose his house because my brother failed to come to court, meaning his bail was forfeited. I asked him how was that possible, when he was in jail at the time of his hearing. I worked for the court system for nine years, so I called the chief judge of the district and asked him how to correct this. He told me how to get it put on the docket, and I filed the proper paperwork.

The day of the hearing I represented my daddy. Believe me my daddy did not have a fool for a lawyer. I was prepared. I presented the case to the judge, finally stating my brother was in jail the day of his hearing. They forgot to bring him to court. The judge looked at the DA, who looked down to say this is true.

The judge dismissed the case, and my daddy and I walked out of the courtroom. I remember an attorney telling me, "You sound like a lawyer." I told him, "You know I worked in the courtroom. After so many years, you pick up the mannerisms." Leaders are born!

BROKEN BUT STILL STANDING

I was born into a church where the pastor preached for fifty-one years that a woman should not be in the pulpit. Well I was convinced of that because that's all I ever heard. The Lord called me to preach in 1996, but I said, "Lord, I'm not going to preach. A woman is not supposed to preach. That's what I've been taught." I ran for three years saying no!

The Devil attacked Stephanie because he knew I loved my children. We began to fight over everything; we just couldn't get along. It got so bad, at the end of the three years (one for the Father, one for the Son, and one for the Holy Spirit) I shouted out to the Lord, "I will do it." And things began to calm down right away.

The Thursday evening before my initial sermon on April 25, 1999, Julian went into the hospital. We got him there just in time to get a spinal tap done. He was hospitalized for eight days with varicella encephalitis. He was in a lethargic state for five of those days and would not speak to the doctors. They told us, "He will probably have brain damage and have to learn how to walk again." I said, "The Devil is a lie! He will not," and I began to pray. I will tell the story later.

By attacking my son, the Devil thought I would not have time to prepare. But it gave me more time to prepare for the coming Sunday. I stayed at the hospital with him five nights and every day. My husband stayed two nights. I brought him home on the eighth day (new beginning).

After my initial sermon, I began to pray for clarity. I prayed, "Lord, what am I to do?" In the middle of the night I saw the word "evangelist" hanging over my bed. I jumped out of the bed, waking Ulysses. He asked, "What are you doing?" "I have to get a dictionary and look up the word 'evangelist'." It said to preach the gospel—the good news.

After that, I didn't care what I had been taught. The Lord had spoken to me, and the dream sealed it for me. Now being I am from a town that does not really care for women pastors, I believed the majority of ministers and pastors thought it was okay for women to preach but not pastor.

After preaching for three years at various churches in and out of town, the persecution and disrespect began, but only in my hometown. We know what the Bible says about being accepted at home. It's true, believe me. I was deeply hurt at my church and my husband's church, where I was a member for fifteen years. I was an outsider, never really accepted, because I wasn't born into that church.

One Sunday I left my home church crying because of the attacks. I heard the Lord say in my spirit, *Now I have moved you into the pastor's office.* When I got home, I ran into the living room and put on a CD. I began to worship the Lord and thank Him. I began to shout. I was tearing up the floor. My husband was in the den. I guess he thought I was crazy. Now I thank those two churches. It was nothing but preparation because I had to be prepared to pastor.

Some family members were upset my family and I left. I am amazed how people think it's good for their family to stick together or stay together but not for other families. God instituted family, and we should all stay together. The family that prays together we know stays together.

I began to seek God about starting a church. The first thing I said was, "I don't want to split a church, Lord. If you're telling me to pastor, let me build a church." That was my request to the Lord. Right away I went and had plans drawn up for a church with seating for 300 (dumb). I even asked for several fleeces from the Lord, and they came to pass. So I found the building and began the task of renovating it into a church. After two months, we had our first service. I spent $12,000 of my own money to get started. I didn't take a salary the first year. The next year I was given a meager salary, which I was fine with because I knew we needed the cash to offset the expenses.

I have a BA degree in business administration from A&T State University. I am wise with money and do not waste it.

I cleaned the entire church for two years to save money for the church. The congregation caught hold of the vision for a new church, and I wanted to build it the first year. It was a little personal for me, because the talk in town was I couldn't do it. And you know what? I could not. But I knew someone who could do it through me. God!

Every year I thought, *Maybe this is the year.* I was eager to get started. By the third year, the Lord spoke to me and said, *It's number five.* I knew what that meant, so I told the congregation we would not move until our fifth year began. Guess what! We began the building project in July—in the fifth year (grace). I was the talk of the town, the most persecuted preacher in town because I was a black woman, founding a church, and I was told the first black woman to pastor in my hometown.

I prayed about the contractor. The architect I hired to lay out the foundation suggested I contact Bryant Inscoe a Christian contractor he knew. I did, and right away we began to receive the favor of God. He didn't charge the normal 25 percent, only 10 percent to build the church.

The loan at the bank went through with ease. Glory to God!

Mind you, I had only had a church for five years, with the land and the building of the church, it cost us $600,000. The church did so well we were able to put down $225,000. The work began, and we had favor from everybody. DOT came and made the driveway. The man said, "I don't know why we are doing sixty feet. We always do forty-five feet."

The well diggers came and said, "We probably will have to go 250 feet." They had just dug a well for my niece and went 250 feet a quarter-mile up ahead. I stretched out my hand and prayed. I told the man, "You won't have to dig that far down here." I left and was not gone thirty minutes before the building contractor called me and said they had hit water.

I turned around and came back. I got out of the car and did a little holy dance, giving God the praise! He said, "I don't know when the last time we hit water at fifty feet." He tested the running rate. I believe it was thirty-two gallons a minute. He said, "You won't ever have to worry about running out of water. You can have car washes if you want to." Look at what God can do if you believe. The water tasted so good I called it holy water.

The contractor who bulldozed the land gave us favor, and the carpenters gave us favor. Extra things were done to the molding to beautify the church at the request of the building contractor. The plumber gave us favor. He put in the most expensive commodes. He said, "I want to do that for you." I was told the inspectors would give us trouble. Not so. They were great. Everything went according to schedule. It was more than I am able to tell you. There's nothing like having favor from God and man.

We had the first church service in our new church on December 27, 2009. We have four entryways, and there is a Bible under the concrete at each door. A dear friend of mine called me and said she had a dream. She was supposed to tell me put a Bible in each corner of the foundation before the concrete was poured. I loved it, but we had already laid the foundation when she told me. The Holy Spirit nudged me and reminded me I had four entrances.

When you walk through the entrance leading to my office, the Bible is open to "The Lord is my Shepherd, I shall not want." When you enter through the double doors in the front of the church, the Bible is open to "Let everything that has breath praise the Lord." The one at the left side door says, "Unless the Lord builds the house the ones who build it labor in vain." The kitchen door Bible is open to "Come let us sing for joy to the Lord; let us shout aloud to the rock of our salvation."

We didn't have funds for a dining hall, and every church needs a dining hall for fellowshipping. So we decided to add on at a later date. I have been asking God for a debt-free church. My prayer is that this book will pay for our new dining hall. I believe God will supply our every need.

Our motto: Come and see
what the Lord has done.

Church Front

Church Sanctuary

Church Side

Church Sign

Close-Up of Bible

Bible at the Door

HEALINGS AND MIRACLES

Iknow God is real because I have seen him in my life! When I look back over my life, I can see where the Devil has tried to kill me three times. I almost drowned in the ocean when I was eighteen. A wave took me. After it passed over and I was trying to compose myself, another wave grabbed me. I felt myself floating. Then I felt a hand grab my swimsuit and bring me in. I always thought Ulysses grabbed me. Now I'm not sure. It may have been my angel.

My van hydroplaned on Interstate 85 and spun around three times in the middle of the road. God held back two transfer trucks until I rested on the guardrail. I thank God for my angels today.

You see, I lost a child twenty-four years ago. I was depressed for five years, smiling on the outside and hurting on the inside. I couldn't pray, and I couldn't read the Bible. I was angry with God because I didn't understand why this was happening. But one day I cried out to God, "God help me." He instantly lifted me from the pit of despair and gave me such peace that I have not mourned her death since that day. Hallelujah!

DALE'S FIGHT FOR LIFE

A couple months after my daughter's death, my sister Audrey Dale was stabbed six times by her boyfriend. Three places the knife hit her should have been fatal, but God saved her. The surgery she had was critical, because she could have had a stroke on the table. It was supposed to take eight hours, it took thirteen. The procedure to repair a vein failed the first time, and they had to do it again. She was in a medically induced coma. Her face was swollen, and she didn't look like herself. She was in the hospital for thirteen days. I only missed one day. I didn't want her to wake up and not be there.

I had pastors and preachers come to pray over her. One pastor disturbed me. Before I took any preacher into the intensive care unit, I told him or her I wanted them to pray for my sister. I knew she could hear a prayer going forth, giving her hope. This preacher and I were back there about ten minutes, and he didn't say anything. She's not awake, so it didn't make sense to just stand there and look at her. I told him, "You can pray now." He said, "I already have." I looked at him and thought *"I didn't hear anything. You need to open your mouth so she can hear you. The doctors say your hearing is the last thing to go."*

When Dale opened her eyes the first thing she said was, "I'm going to Sunday school." She was always in church. I said, "Dale, don't make a vow to God that you can't keep." She had heard those prayers because she woke up with Jesus on her mind. She recovered. And though the doctors said she probably wouldn't be able to talk well because her jugular vein had been cut, she's the first one in Sunday school every Sunday and sings in the choir. Dale has a beautiful alto voice. Look what God can do when you call on Him and believe. I believe prayer was the answer for her.

MY MOTHER'S DEATH

When my mother developed kidney failure, her doctor told her she would not live four months if she didn't go on dialysis. She refused to go on dialysis, so I had to make sure she was saved. I led her in to salvation, the greatest miracle we will ever experience. Five years later she had a heart attack in the grocery store. Two weeks later she's died. The week before she died, she told me she loved me. I knew she did, but it was a blessing to hear it.

My sister Sylvia and I were at a church, and an elderly woman, one of our mother's friends, came up to me. She said, "Your mother told me that you said God would forgive us for our sins. I don't drink anymore." I said, "He will if you mean it." That really blessed my soul. My momma helped somebody get saved.

NITA'S DEATH

One year later, my sister Nita went to the beach for the weekend. She came back in a hearse. We had to shift our grief from our mother to our sister. I had her son, eighteen-month-old Julian, in my day care that Friday. She pulled out of the driveway and then came back. I asked Nita why she came back. She said, "I can't leave Julian." I wonder if she felt something because she was leaving him for good.

This was bike week at the beach, and the law did not require you to wear a helmet. She was on the back of a motorcycle, and a sixteen-year-old pulled out and hit the bike. She was thrown into the air and slammed down on the concrete. About three o'clock in the morning, my cousin called and said Nita had been in an accident. I asked her if it was bad, and she said she thought so. I said, "She'll be all right." My cousin repeated it looked pretty bad. I told her to call me back and let me know what was happening.

My brother Randall, Sylvia, and a cousin Willie T. were at the hospital with Nita. I don't recall whether her son Rajaun was at the hospital, but he was also at the beach. At three thirty I got a call from the doctor. He said it looked bad. I asked if she had brain damage, and he said yes. He also said she was broken up pretty badly. The doctor said, "We want to know if you want to pull the plug." I'm wondering, *Why didn't he call my daddy to do that?* I asked, "There's nothing you can do for her?" He said no. I breathed in deeply and said, "Pull the plug."

He called me back thirty minutes later and said, "She's gone." I called the funeral home. It's one thing to expect someone who is sick or old to die, but when you're vibrant, happy, and thirty-five and leave home, we expect for you to come back.

This was a shock to our family. Nita was the first sibling to die in our family. Nobody believed it. It was like a dream we wanted somebody to wake us up. Only when we went to the private viewing did we believe it. When we got to door of the funeral home, no one wanted to go in. I told my brother, who was the oldest, to go in. He stepped back, so I went in first.

Nita was in the first viewing room. I peeped around the corner and just hollered and cried when I saw her. We all did. The owner walked away with tears in his eyes. Nita had dated his son. His wife came and grabbed me. We were pitiful.

MY DADDY'S DEATH

Most of my life I prayed and asked God to let my daddy live to see seventy-two years of age. I don't know where that number came from; I just did it. I said it so much I found myself about to say it when he was dead. Just like I would pick up the phone to call my momma, and she was dead.

When he turned seventy-one, he had a stroke and heart attack. I had sent prayers up for my daddy, all those years, now I understood why I was praying that way. The doctor said he had five blocked arteries; three were operable and two inoperable. I told the doctor, "We will take the medicine." I'm talking for my daddy because I now know the authority I have in Jesus' name.

Sitting on his hospital bed, I led him into salvation. I thought, *If he gets upset with me he was already in the hospital.* It's not an easy thing to lead your daddy into salvation. He's the head of the house. But I was determined nobody in my family is going to hell if I can help it.

So at church one Sunday night, I asked those who believed in healing to come and agree with me for my daddy's healing. I asked God to open his arteries in the name of Jesus. I never thought about it anymore.

A lot of times we miss what God does for us. The last eighteen months of his life were spent in the rest home. I would go in his room, and he would be lying flat in the bed, with no pillow behind his head. So I put a pillow behind his head. God was showing me something, but I missed it. They hooked him up to heart monitors for two weeks, and the doctor said his heart was fine. I still missed what God was showing me.

Only in prayer after he died a few years later did God let me know He did what I asked; my daddy's arteries were open. If you have five blocked arteries, you cannot lie flat on your back, because you can't breathe in that position. But my daddy did. He never complained about shortness of breath. I have a story to tell if anyone will listen. God will do just what He said He will do.

I walked in his room one day, and he had started panting. I went over to the bed and said it's time daddy, don't be afraid to cross over. I walked out the room and looked back at him, it was a strange feeling. I knew he was leaving us. As I was leaving my sister Sylvia was coming we locked eyes passing in our cars. By the time she got in his room, he was gone. He panted one day. He left here peacefully, a sweet death. The doctors at the hospital told me my mother also left peacefully, with a smile on her face. Look what prayer can do. You can't make me doubt God. I know too much about Him!

Our father and our mother both lived five years after giving their lives to Christ. Five means grace (unmerited favor). They didn't deserve it, and their time may have been up earlier. But because we serve a good God, He gave them favor.

JULIAN'S HOSPITAL VISIT

Eight days before I was to give my initial sermon, my son, Julian, after Nita's death I adopted him, he entered the hospital for eight days. He was in critical condition, and the Devil tried to take him out. Let me tell you why you can't make me doubt God. He was diagnosed with the chickenpox virus, varicella encephalitis. When I got him there, they rushed him in and gave him a spinal tap. The doctors said, "You got him here just in time."

Over the next three days, Julian had an EEG—all those wires hooked to his head—two MRIs and a CAT scan. Before every test, I anointed him in the name of Jesus. All the tests came back negative.

The doctors were concerned because all he did was sleep for three days. When they came in, they couldn't get him to stand up by himself; he couldn't feed himself. He had all the symptoms of the virus, but the doctors couldn't find it in his body. They were sure he would have brain damage. I rebuked that! They said he would have to learn how to walk all over again, and it would take three months of rehab. I rebuked that! I never doubted he would get well, because I knew the Devil was behind the sickness, and God had given me such peace about Julian, I didn't care what the doctors said.

The strangest thing happened. Julian would talk to me but never to the doctors. When they observed him, he just lay there and wouldn't do anything for them. This is what made them think he had brain damage. But God would let him talk to me, letting me know he was all right. When the doctors left the room, I would ask Julian, "Do you know who I am?" And he would say, "Yes, my momma." I would ask him his colors, pointing to them, and he would say them.

One night he told me he saw a man standing behind me. I turned around and looked. No one was there. I said, "Julian, there's no one behind me." Then he said, "I see your baby." Mind you, my daughter had been dead for nine years, and Julian was only three years old. She was dead before he was born, so how could he possibly know I had a daughter who died? He got my attention then.

It scared me, and I started rebuking the spirit in the room. Suddenly, something hit me in my stomach. It was the Holy Spirit, reminding me of the prayer I had said asking God to send an angel to protect Julian. I knew who the man was then. Julian could see him and my daughter, but I could not. God put him in a stupor because demons only attack what moves. They can't do anything with a dead body or a still one.

Shelby and Roy came in the room, and I left to visit someone else in the hospital. When I came back, they said Julian had told them the same thing. I believe children can sometimes see into the spiritual realm better than we can. I told my husband, "I will be glad when Sunday comes because he will wake up." And he did Sunday afternoon.

The Devil thought Julian's illness would distract me from preparing for my sermon. What it really did was give me more time to study. I sat with him all day and all night, studying.

They sent him to rehab on Wednesday to learn how to walk. All day Thursday they did nothing but play with him. I couldn't help but think about the mounting hospital costs. We had just put him on our insurance two months before he got sick and we didn't know if it had kicked in. The court gave me custody in 1998 when he was 3 years old.

I told the hospital social worker and doctor I wanted to take him home. What they were doing I could do at home. They said no. I told them I believed that God would heal him. I looked at my watch; it was 8 p.m. I left the hospital and headed for my Bible study group. I had seen miracles and healings take place in the home of Steve and Mary Downey. I had been in that Bible study group for ten years. The pastor was anointed to teach us the Bible. As they were leaving around nine thirty, I told Pastor Morgan, "I want you all to touch and agree with me that God will strengthen Julian's legs."

On Thursday, Julian couldn't stand by himself. I want you to know that when I walked in there Friday, he ran to me. He walked in three days instead of three months. The social worker said, "We don't know what happened." I yelled, "I do. It's God! He has God's healing power on him. And I want to take him home."

The staff was amazed, and the doctors were baffled. They didn't understand. But I did. It was God. A miracle had taken place. Seeing Julian walk, they wanted to keep him there three more days. I said, "No, I will not dishonor God by letting him stay here."

Two doctors and the social worker tried to convince me he needed treatment. He didn't need any more treatment. They were just interested in statistical data. He had the best doctor of all time—Dr. Jesus.

By the time I got through telling them about the goodness of God and what He had done for Julian, they were signing papers to release him to go home that evening. The doctor looked at me and said, "You have strong faith, and I said, it's because I know the God I serve can do anything. All things are possible if you believe. I'm a believer!"

They made me promise to bring him back for an eye/ear exam in two weeks. When taking him back for the examinations, I prayed all the way: "Saying God, I know You have healed him. I'm just doing this to pacify the doctors and because I gave my word." Both checkups were good. The eye doctor asked me why, did I bring Julian in, to check his eyes because he had perfect vision. I told her the doctor made the appointment. His hearing test was also normal.

When I got the hospital bill, it was $18,000. After the insurance paid what was covered, the balance was $2,700. I sent in $100. When the payment didn't show up on the bill, I called the hospital. The automated voice kept saying adjustments had been made to the bill, and the new balance was $460. I quickly dropped that check in the mail. I call that a supernatural blessing from the Lord. We serve an awesome God!

A miracle is something you have to work. At two thirty one morning, I got a call letting me know a member in the church was sick and could not be awakened. I woke Ulysses, and we went to the house. On the way I prayed, asking God to give me a sign he was all right.

When I walked into the bedroom, his wife and children were around the bed, crying, and the EMTs were working frantically. I noticed he was moving, lifting himself off the bed. That was my sign!

The EMTs yelled out, "Somebody hold him down." They were trying to get a needle in his arm. The fact he was moving too much broke the needle as the EMT tried to stick it in his arm. Blood splattered everywhere, and his wife hollered out.

I looked at the family and realized they couldn't do anything. They were too emotional. At that moment I thought, *Somebody has to hold him down.* A son was already on the bed, at his father's left side. I hollered to him, "Hold him still." He said, "Daddy, be still," with tears running down his eyes. I will never forget that, because he said it so tenderly. When he pushed down on his daddy, he did it so softly his father was still lifting himself up.

I jumped on the bed, straddled him, and put both my hands on his knees, locking them in position. An EMT hollered, "Can I get on the bed?" I said yes. He came over to the right side of me. Again I told the son to hold his daddy down, but he just couldn't push down hard on his daddy. I stretched out over his father and pushed down on his left shoulder. I began to speak in tongues. I heard the Holy Spirit say, *Put your hand on his heart.* So I moved my right hand from his shoulder to his heart. I stayed with the tongues. Suddenly, the EMT hollered, "I got it." He was excited and glad.

Instantly, he began to calm down. As I backed up to get off of him, he became alert and wondered what was going on. I know he was wondering why his pastor was at the foot of the bed, straddling his legs.

I got down and asked the EMT, "Does he need to go to the hospital?" He said, "He can go, but all they're going to do is give him something to eat." I said, "We can do that here." The EMT told me to get him a glass of tea or orange juice with a spoonful of sugar in it and then give him something to eat. The food was prepared for him and he was eating breakfast at 4:30 in the morning. We left. And guess who entered the church doors the next day. He did.

His son called me Sunday morning and told me the EMT told him his daddy's organs had begun to shut down. It was his pacemaker that helped him. I said, "Praise God! That's why the Holy Spirit told me to put my hand on his heart." To God be the glory!

The Devil tried to take him out that night. His wife worked third shift but decided not to go in that night. She thought that was her decision. I believe it was the leading of the Holy

Spirit. If she had gone to work, no one would have known he was having a diabetic incident. He would not be here today.

That was seven years ago, and he is still here. We praised the Lord that morning in the church service, giving God the glory for his life. When he walked in the door I said, "Here comes my Lazarus.

Another miracle I saw before my eyes occurred with my aunt. My cousin called and said her mother was down in her back, couldn't get out of the bed, and was in a lot of pain. I told my cousin I would go to the house and check on her mother.

When I got there, I knocked on the door. It was locked, so I could not get in. I called her, and she answered the telephone. I could hear her pain in her voice. I asked if she could get up and open the door. She said, "I can't move." I asked her how I could get into the house. She said, "I don't know. I can't get up." So I called my cousin, who was working at the hospital, and told her to come and let me in. She said Lena was on her way and would let me in.

When she came I went into the bedroom, and my aunt and I talked about what she was experiencing. I told her I was going to anoint her back in the name of Jesus and pray for her. If she believed the prayer offered to God, she would be healed.

After I prayed, I told her to bend her leg, and she did it. Then I told her to sit up. When she did that instantly, she was healed in the name of Jesus. And she got out of bed and stood without help.

Her daughter walked into the room and said, "Mom, you're standing up!" Lena began to cry because she knew the pain her mother was in and that she could not get out of the bed. But all things are possible if you believe!

It's sad to say, but many Christians don't believe in the healing power of Jesus. You preach it from the pulpit, and the people will witness (Amen), but they believe it in their heads and not in their hearts. When my aunt bent her leg, she believed she was healed. And that's just what she got—a healing.

If you ask God for something but don't really believe it will happen, stop praying. It will not manifest in your life. Without faith, prayers are seldom answered because it's the prayer of faith that brings about a change in your life or the life of the person you pray for.

Yes, I believe you can have faith for the babes in Christ or the sinner to get them saved. But sooner or later, they will have to stand on their own faith. We have to believe we are healed by the stripes of Jesus. We have to believe Jesus took our sin and sickness with him to the cross.

FUNNY STORIES

There is a funny story when I first went in the ministry. I went to a funeral at a holy church. I don't know why we say that. Aren't all churches supposed to be holy?

The preachers were lined up for the funeral procession; there were nine of them. A woman who was ushering came over and told me I was in the wrong line. She pointed to the flower girls, letting me know I was supposed to be over there. I smiled and said, "I'm in the right line." The bishop was behind me, last in the line. I looked at him, and we laughed.

I got to the pulpit, and there were nine seats, just enough for the men. So the pastor came down to meet me before I entered in the pulpit. He was not going to let me come in his pulpit. He asked me, "Do you mind sitting next to the piano." I said I didn't mind. I didn't care where

I sat as long as he found me a seat. The church was full.

They placed a seat beside the piano, and the pastor waved for Bishop Betts to come in the pulpit. There was one seat left. He told the pastor, "Put me a chair down here. I'll sit here," pointing to where I sat. He could have made me feel like an outcast, but because of his humble spirit, he did what he thought was right. I have the utmost respect for him as a preacher of the gospel. His wife is one of my best friends.

I saw the woman usher years later and asked if she remembered that incident. She did, and we both laughed about it. Why should I get mad at her? She had been taught a woman didn't belong in the pulpit. So she just knew I was in the wrong line.

One Saturday night I was at my sister-in-law's house. A car sped in to the driveway, and another car followed. A white man got out of the first car, ran to the door, and said, "Help me or let me in. Someone is following me."

You need to know my sister-in-law lived up north for many years. Whenever I went to her house, the storm door was locked, especially at night. She opened the door, and the man tried to rush past her. She began to push the door against him and hollered for her daughter to help her. There they were, pushing him out, and he was pushing in, asking them to let him in.

It was so funny. They looked scared to death. After it was over, we just laughed. Ulysses said, "You should have helped the man." She said he was not coming in her house.

I can't remember how we found out what was going on. I think they were arguing outside in the yard. But we do know the man trying to get into the house had the other man's wife with him. Her husband was playing detective, and his hunch paid off. The fact they kept the man out was a good thing. That situation could have turned ugly inside her house. We laughed for about thirty minutes about that incident. And the very same scenario would have played out, if it was a black man so color did not have anything to do with it.

There are times when, something can happen and it can be serious at the moment, but after it's over and you reflect on what happened.

You can see that it was a little funny, especially if no one is hurt.

How often have you passed someone walking, needing a ride, and you didn't pick up the person. That was a sin of neglect. So before you judge them, think about yourself. How many times have you not helped someone because of fear? That's the world we live in today.

FAVORITE PROVERBS

The key word in Proverbs is "wisdom," "the ability to live life skillfully." A godly life in an ungodly world, however, is no simple assignment. Proverbs provides God's detailed instructions for His people to deal successfully with the practical affairs of everyday life. I would like to share some of my favorite proverbs, and I pray you receive wisdom and apply them to your life. (All are from the *New International Version* of the Holy Bible.)

The fear of the Lord is the beginning of knowledge, but fools despise wisdom and discipline. (Proverbs 1:7)

My son, do not forget my teaching, but keep my commands in your heart, for they will prolong your life many years and bring you prosperity. Let love and faithfulness never leave you; bind them around your neck, write them on the tablet of your heart. Then you will win favor and a good name in the sight of God and man. Trust in the Lord with all your heart and lean not to your own understanding; in all your ways acknowledge him, and he will make your paths straight. Do not be wise in your own eyes; fear the Lord and shun evil. This will bring health to your body and nourishment to your bones. (Proverbs 3:1–8)

My son, do not despise the Lord's discipline and do not resent his rebuke, because the Lord disciplines those he loves, as a father the son he delights in. (Proverbs 3:11–12)

Do not accuse a man for no reason when he has done you no harm. (Proverbs 3:30)

The Lord's curse is on the house of the wicked but he blesses the home of the righteous. (Proverbs 3:33)

There are six things the Lord hates, seven that are detestable to him: haughty eyes, a lying tongue, hands that shed innocent blood, a heart that devises wicked schemes, feet that are quick to rush into evil, a false witness who pours out lies and a man who stirs up dissension among brothers. (Proverbs 6:16–19)

Do not rebuke a mocker or he will hate you; rebuke a wise man and he will love you. Instruct a wise man and he will be wiser still; teach a righteous man and he will add to his learning. (Proverbs 9:8–9)

Lazy hands make a man poor, but diligent hands bring wealth. (Proverbs 10:4)

The memory of the righteous will be a blessing but the name of the wicked will rot. (Proverbs 10:7)

The man of integrity walks securely, but he who takes crooked paths will be found out. (Proverbs 10:9)

He who heeds discipline shows the way to life, but whoever ignores correction leads others astray. He who conceals his hatred has lying lips, and whoever spreads slander is a fool. (Proverbs 10:17–18)

The blessing of the Lord brings wealth, and he adds no trouble to it. (Proverbs 10:22)

What the wicked dread will overtake them; what the righteous desire will be granted. (Proverbs 10:24)

Be sure of this: The wicked will not go unpunished, but those who are righteous will go free. (Proverbs 11:21)

A truthful witness gives honest testimony, but a false witness tells lies. (Proverbs 12:17)

No harm befalls the righteous, but the wicked have their fill of trouble. The Lord detests lying lips, but he delights in men who are truthful. (Proverbs 12:21–22)

Dishonest money dwindles away, but he who gathers money little by little makes it grows. (Proverbs 13:11)

A good man leaves an inheritance for his children's children, but a sinner's wealth is stored up for the righteous. (Proverbs 13:22)

He who spares the rod hates his son, but he who loves him is careful to discipline him. (Proverbs 13:24)

A truthful witness does not deceive, but a false witness pours out lies. (Proverbs 14:5)

The house of the wicked will be destroyed, but the tent of the upright will flourish. There is a way that seems right to a man, but in the end it leads to death. (Proverbs 14:11–12)

All hard work brings a profit, but mere talk leads only to poverty. (Proverbs 14:23)

The eyes of the Lord are everywhere, keeping watch on the wicked and the good. (Proverbs 15:3)

When a man ways are pleasing the Lord, he makes even his enemies live at peace with him. (Proverbs 16:7)

A perverse man stirs up dissension, and a gossip separates close friends. (Proverbs 16:28)

If a man pays back evil for good, evil will never leave his house. (Proverbs 17:13)

Even a fool is thought wise if he keeps silent, and discerning if he holds his tongue. (Proverbs 17:28)

Before his downfall a man's heart is proud, but humility comes before honor. (Proverbs 18:12)

The tongue has the power of life and death, and those who love it will eat its fruit. He who finds a wife finds what is good and receives favor from the Lord. (Proverbs 18:21–22)

He who is kind to the poor lends to the Lord, and he will reward him for what he has done. (Proverbs 19:17)

A gossip betrays a confidence; so avoid a man who talks too much. If a man curses his father and mother, his lamp will be snuffed out in pitch darkness. (Proverbs 20:19–20)

To do what is right and just is more acceptable to the Lord than sacrifice. (Proverbs 21:3)

He who loves pleasure will become poor; whoever loves wine and oil will never be rich. (Proverbs 21:17)

Humility and the fear of the Lord bring wealth and honor and life. (Proverbs 22:4)

Train a child in the way he should go, and when he is old he will not turn from it. (Proverbs 22:6)

Do not withhold discipline from a child; if you punish him with the rod, he will not die. Punish him with the rod and save his soul from death. (Proverbs 23:13–14)

An honest answer is like a kiss on the lips. (Proverbs 24:26)

If your enemy is hungry, give him food to eat; if he is thirsty, give him water to drink. In doing this, you will heap burning coals on his head and the Lord will reward you. (Proverbs 25:21–22)

A malicious man disguises himself with his lips, but in his heart he harbors deceit. Though his speech is charming, do not believe him, for seven abominations fill his heart. His malice may be concealed by deception, but his wickedness will be exposed in the assembly. If a man digs a pit, he will fall into it; if a man rolls a stone, it will roll back on him. A lying tongue hates those it hurts and a flattering mouth works ruin. (Proverbs 26:24–28)

Do not boast about tomorrow, for you do not know what a day may bring forth. Let another praise you, and not your own mouth; someone else, and not your own lips. (Proverbs 27:1–2)

Better is open rebuke than hidden love. Wounds from a friend can be trusted but an enemy multiplies kisses. (Proverbs 27:5–6)

He who leads the upright along an evil path will fall into his own trap but the blameless will receive a good inheritance. (Proverbs 28:10)

He who conceals his sins does not prosper, but whoever confesses and renounces them finds mercy. (Proverbs 28:13)

A man's pride brings him low, but a man of lowly spirit gains honor. (Proverbs 29:23)

The righteous detest the dishonest; the wicked detest the upright. (Proverbs 29:27)

Every word of God is flawless; he is a shield to those who take refuge in him. Do not add to his words, or he will rebuke you and prove you a liar. (Proverbs 30:5–6)

Speak up for those who cannot speak for themselves, for the rights of all who are destitute. Speak up and judge fairly; defend the rights of the poor and needy. (Proverbs 31:8–9)

ABOUT THE AUTHOR

CHARLENE EVANS MORTON is the founder and senior pastor of Greater Harvest Full Gospel Baptist Church in Oxford, North Carolina. She is the first black woman to pastor and build a church in her hometown. The doors of the church opened September 7, 2003. She believes the most important thing in life is receiving salvation in the name of Jesus. She is a 1976 graduate of A&T State University in Greensboro, North Carolina. She is married to Ulysses, and they have four children—Shelby, Stephanie, Julian, and Rajaun—four grandchildren—Marcelous, Roy, Faith, and Rhythm—and a son-in-law, Roy Hunt.

To God be the glory for the things He has done!